MARK FLECKENSTEIN

Making Up The World

First published by Editions Dedicaces in 2018

Copyright © Mark Fleckenstein, 2018

All rights reserved. No part of this publication may be reproduced, stored or transmitted in any form or by any means, electronic, mechanical, photocopying, recording, scanning, or otherwise without written permission from the publisher. It is illegal to copy this book, post it to a website, or distribute it by any other means without permission.

First edition

ISBN: 978-1-77076-719-5

This book was professionally typeset on Reedsy. Find out more at reedsy.com

I wish to thank the Massachusetts Arts Lottery Council, whose financial support enabled me to complete some of these poems.

Special thanks to Karen Bjorkman, Zeynep Beykont, Lori Byrne, Gloria Mindock, Carl Phillips, Catherine Sasanov and Dzvinia Orlowsky whose friendship, encouragement, and criticism helped make many of these poems possible.

For Karen Bjorkman

Contents

Acknowledgement   iii
    iv

Always Begin Where You Are   1
Two Sides Of The Same Fence   3
Improvisation   6
Prelude   7
Name That Tune   10
One Never Knows What One Might   12
The End's A Beginning That's Lost Its Way   14
If Not For You   17
As You Were Saying   18
Winter Travel   19
Wonder   21
Repetition   23
Angels   25
Mirror   27
Upstairs   28
Ex Libris   29
Art Gallery Pension   31
Travelling Light   34
Traveling By Albatross   35
Another Page Illustrated By Fire   36
Bones Covered With Breath   37
Necessary Angels   38
Hourglass-Memory   39

The Music Dreams Make Of Empty Rage	40
Insomnia Meditation	41
Initiation	42
Divergent Perspectives	43
The Distance Between Memory And Remembering	44
Business Travel	45
Migration	47
Emergency Lane	48
Triptych: The Art Of Perspective	49
Making Up The World	51
Notes	55

Acknowledgement

Grateful acknowledgement to the editors of the following publications where some of these poems, often very different versions, first appeared:

BLuR (Boston Literary Review): "Making Up The World"

Sticks: "Another Page Illustrated By Fire"

If you know the right combination of letters, you can make anything. This is the secret power of the alphabet. Meaningless sounds, abstract symbols, they have the power of creation. This is why the various parts of the mystical writings are not in proper order. Knowing the order, you could make your own world from just reading the writings. Everything is built from the 22 letter elements. The alphabet itself is both male and female. Creation depends on an anagram.
— *Don DeLillo,* **Ratner's Star**

Always Begin Where You Are

1

—

My memory of you lacks perspective,
the ability to blink, and well-defined
colors. A shadow in a veiled mirror,
my memory of you begins and ends
like a pair of loaded dice.

This is the suit I wore:
double-breasted black flannel.
Chalk striped and out of style.
The pocket watch, the eyeglasses,
the hole in each shoe, the small deaths
of late afternoon, and early evening.
Hours become days, then years,
then absent, and irreversible.

2

—

Begin again with another letter,
a smile borrowed from your neighbor,
stolen shoes, shortness of breath,
a room resuscitated by fire,

the night you passed through my fingers
like a pair of sacred bones
turned into so much dust after
years of ritual gesticulation.

3

The face in the mirror
confides in its reflection —
if you are truly not in despair,
you must at every moment destroy
the possibility — answering
the question left in the other room
like an unmailed letter —

this is not despair.
If you're like the rest of us,
this is what you remember.
If you're like the rest of us,
you no longer know anything
but how to breathe and blink.

Otherwise, you should be dressed for mourning.

Two Sides Of The Same Fence

1
—

Less the need to travel, the realization
that money has its own weather,

evenings spent too drunk to know what
argument to raise, the percussive

saxophone of a cross-street neighbor;
your hair softly brown and longer,

this could have been our story:

"If a train leaves Boston for San Diego
at 6:47 a.m. going 137 miles an hour

and a train leaves San Diego for Boston
at 9:43 a.m. going 141 miles an hour, when

do they not collide but with one suitcase
in each hand and lonely smile, arrive?"

2
—

From a room where two half-opened curtains
display a sanded-down moon, and dying rose

having turned away a series of years
and memories the thickness of moonlight

and water, there's nothing in the world
beyond the cup of coffee, I just threw out.

One-footed, left-handed, soft, and rotten
with light, my days are not unlike yours.

Nothing much bad ever seems to happen.
With the sun less than halfway down

the back of late afternoon, rain
polishes the streets to a black shimmer,

thins the air and draws us out of hiding.

3.
—

There's pleasure in these quieter days,
in not thinking of our separation

as anything more than miles and lies.
Where you've settled, all arguments

become numeric: Whose turn
is it to take out the garbage?

When will this day end?
How soon will you be leaving?

Your life has changed. Late fall.
Wind shifting, crisp, arrogant, free.

On this side of the gate you forgot how it feels.

Improvisation

Friends of this life or another, I am powerful tired. My skin yawns. The sandman's dump truck broke down in my hair. My dreams aren't unpleasant but need a twist tie and garbage bag, at least. It is nothing so much as not much more than sunlight's striptease for undulating clouds and carefully blue sky not wanting to spoil its brow. To think, ah yes, to dream, now that is a question. I slept pretty as a dinosaur on the train tracks yesterday and may tomorrow but today, it wouldn't feel right. Clothes make a man and mine are borrowed. Facts are sad. Without them, it's fish meal again, or maybe Friday but most likely Tuesday, the ambiguous. I'll not go gentle, extinction by committee, the way of the dodo, straight up or down a fire pole ladder named Jacob, Angel, Archimedes, Gregor, Mary, Heraclitus. Plain as smoke and even tempted. Going, going, go.

Prelude

In three weeks, we'll witness
    the rebirth of Western Civilization.

    Scale model versions predict the event
in asphyxiating detail and include

floats decorated with plastic snow,
Vaseline smiling beauty queens

soft shouldered from waving,
bad directions for tourists seeking

the optimal parade viewing point,
the sign in front of our house —

On a day not unlike this somewhere
in the Midwest, the world we know began

and two tiny figurines lock-stepped
in silence. In the house fourteen steps east

of there, someone left the kitchen window
open. A desperate prayer ("The horror,

friends, the eternal horror show of sin")
bleats from the radio. There's also a piano,

no animals and two pictures too small
to be anything but visual noise.

One is blue, unframed and Rothko-like.
The other, the color of your eyes.

When and if you arrive, it will be
with the studied grace of higher math.

The parakeets whose invisible songs
decorate the lack of trees belong

to the neighbors you always refer
to as "oh, them." But let's not

change the subject. If I recall
your tale of a sweatery waltz

on an evening cold and dark enough
to have been real, began and ended

This isn't about my life.
I never lived there —

then became an angry red mouthful
when the rumors turned true —

this was where you grew up.
If the phone rings again,

PRELUDE

it will be you saying —
I was only joking. Please let me come home.

That's the version of our history
you parade before friends and strangers

leaving me to add *that's really
what happened.* So, when you arrive

loaded down with Chinese take-out
and lipstick on your collar,

I'll not disappoint you. If only
I knew what you think I know.

But like a bald man who every morning
remembers not to comb his hair,

I've grown adept at telling stories
that incorporate absence. If history

is written by the victorious,
the losers still get the best lines.

Name That Tune

If I live long enough, the clouds
  will take on the shape of all
  the prayers I've thrown at them
and begin to resemble the snapped
thread of my heart and the safety
pin bent beyond usefulness that would
replace it. History is another name
for how objects misunderstand each other.
Ours began with flowers and the failed
quest of one voice to make articulated
arms of lips, to dissolve the barrier
between object and name. It could
have been the day I ceased believing
that faith, a pinprick of belief
in anything smaller than your absence,
would become sensible if I waited
long enough. It could have been.

The wind is slamming rain against
the windows and will continue
long enough to give the flowers
a chance to make it through summer.
Like all my prayers, this one starts
with the same grimace of vowels
meant to replicate longing and ends

before it gets any further than
the streetlight's hum of undeclared love
for the curtains, Coltrane's meditations
on the conundrum of faith, my memory
of your hair tinseled with morning
light and sleep. It is the song
that keeps the world in place by hiding
our prayers beneath its pillow
until they ask the right question.
If I live long enough, the years
before I got here, when anything
could have been, will have returned.
With the sound of your voice lighting
the room, the years I thought I'd burned
through will have become cool and safe
as early evening. In the double-breasted
suit and stylish tie I imagined success
would wear, I'll preen before the full-
length mirror that softens my name
until we're a near-perfect fit.
Luck the strange shadow falling shy
of embrace behind me.

One Never Knows What One Might

Was it the desire for spring falling
against our end of the world or
a three-week snowstorm that began
the condensed version of our life
together? I remember you said *we
should go on* and thinking it would
mean a favorable twist in the wind
or maybe dive-bombing the sheets.
If you were to again tell me every-
thing, the *eureka* of our history
would not treat us with another made-
for-TV movie score, but an exotic
name for the tea leaves cursed
with our fortune. The outcome's
the same: nothing ever quite works.
Our conversations — *you were wearing
beige and black* — *I was trapped
in English and four other languages.
Chicken salad, tuna salad… they
had everything* — are shuffled and
re-shuffled, safer a little, in
slippers and lamplit. The curtains
arc and ebb. This year promised
the rebirth of romance would replace
the past decade's lust for singularity,

financial stamina, coordinated kitchen
cabinets and the perfect afternoon
martini — vermouth glancing the gin,
sunlight piercing ice. If we were
to take all the days we meant
to each other, make up their
faces, throw wardrobe leftovers
at their feet, breathe Midwestern
accents into them, what would we
do then? Would we know what to do?
Lately, everything seems possible.
I could easily unravel another year
in this apartment where the light
that began the world will end
or go away and forget where I've
come from. There's no turning back
to anything other than what looms
ahead. Wherever you go, there you
are. That any life should offer
such blushes of immortality.

The End's A Beginning That's Lost Its Way

1
—

Nothing's changed. The daily bump
and grind of weather covers most
of whatever I could tell you.
A hard edge and soft moon marks
these nights as they spill across
the light blue shirt I'll iron
for work. By the time this finds
you, I'll have gone back to bed
and awakened in the same dirty light
I found this morning. My last letter
began "Remember that time I stole
flowers from a street vendor" then
digressed into commentary on the lives
we'd invented for different occasions:
the one meant for England; before that,
Uruguay; then Turkey. These days
linger between radio blasts from
passing cars and hints of more
to living than two arms, a new coat
no place special to go; and pass
like a blind man trying to make change
in a foreign currency. My memories

of you, of neighbor's whose arguments
drowned out Glen Miller's "String of Pearls"
have grown two sizes too small
and fit comfortably inside a pocket-
worn envelope. The post office closed
before I could mail you this black
and white postcard of main street
America (circa 1947): Roadmasters
and Packards parked diagonally
in front of Ben Franklin's Five &
Dime, the "I love bargains" banner
clouding the gray and white sky.

2

Maybe the way one hand talks back
to the darkness isn't romantic;

the language it uses will never
seduce a shadow to let unflawed

color spread against its curves.
If you still believe this day is

the first of the rest of your life,
avoid store windows and alcohol.

Wait for the telephone not to ring,
for darkness to stretch the room

larger than the hands of any would-
be lover. In seven years this run

of luck will dissolve among newly-forged
friends into loud talk and laughter

about years lost in too much reflection.
The first night of that month's full moon,

you'll wish for their happiness
then rip out the telephone

after calling Seattle, Columbus
and Boston when no one's home.

By late morning, you'll mistake how
sunlight fills the room for voices.

And swear if you hear them again, you'll answer.

If Not For You

Energy weighs less than thought, hence
light's fluidity and frequency of irascible indecision.
Even now, less, after all, is it not, less. And the ice broken,
the door open to appease the welter anticipated
from the office next to the print shop. A convenience,
like a desktop lunch catered but from the wrong menu.
What to make all this hurly-burly, this hub-bub?
It's the wrong season, but who's counting. "Let's go, boys."
A perfect time to visit the Adirondacks, blouse up a picnic
and call in sick. That Friday afternoon flu. Her car
wouldn't start, something about a prediction of rain,
possibly snow, yet she can barely read. The clouds
would tell a different story, but not right now. It's
just like you said, your perfectly white shirt buttoned
to the collar and close enough to choke, although a pastel
blue or faint pink, however daring, would be more pleasing.
It's cumbersome, geologically. Which one goes that way?
I forgave your prurient assignation, remonstrating feebly, ad
nauseum, roguish as spent cigars and as if you didn't
already know like a mechanical fortuneteller, one card
down and three to go. But hurry up it's time. The fog
will ramble in an hour or more, and then we'll be stuck
like a pair of umbrellas, poised for a punch line.

As You Were Saying

The weather's petulant, passive-aggressive silence
like wire shirt hangers only punctuates my premise:
when the ducks arrive, v-ing across the horizon,
an amelodic harmony intended to infuriate the rocks
by the pond, will confuse the prognostications
of the Farmers' Almanac. You grabbed your coat
as if go, but where? Somebody has to mind the store,
keep the wolves in order and polite. Of course, it's Spring,
but let's not change the subject. It's your turn to serve,
and volley. The hotel room is unobtrusive, smaller
than advertised like the aged outline of a long missing
mirror. Travel is always a crapshoot; the food, fellow
guests like pages hand-shredded from the yellow pages.
Forget the phone. Anyone who knows where we've
gone, would dial the wrong number and the fire trucks
arrive like flat tires awaiting AAA, before the gas tank
goes dead. Self-knowledge is like another week,
the landscape, visitors and names of the animals, domestic
and otherwise ill-remembered and vexing. Hints of dark
spells splayed and filleted expertly. We should have
known better, or did you already? A trick of the wrist,
you meant to say, but it was really the wallpaper, again
fashionable tufted velvet, not a hint of Elvis anywhere,
but soon. When you get there, let me know. I'll send flowers.

Winter Travel

Fingers making up the back, slimming
the thighs, tightening the buttocks,
the lower torso, breasts, etc.,
a picture window view of water
and water and water, the sky nearly
wrung of all light, this is the music
that should be playing. That you're
better looking a year later and even
better after ten is no surprise.
A greased palm is everything
Here — you'd never know it
by the look of things. Service
was promised at 7:00. By the end
of the century, change will be
the only thing turning the key.
You never thought we'd make anything
of ourselves but two chairs
pointed at opposing sunrises.

The alternative life, spent in
foreign currencies, never seemed
real, despite the photographs.
Was it always this way? One hill
then another, insistent and inane
clouds chattering above age-softened

mountains and meadows, a lingering
Schubert piano theme the only thing
not quite present. After years
of worrying the stars, of wondering
were they too old to be anywhere
but where they'd died, long after
dusk and dreams of dining on a black
sand beach in Thailand, your smile
began and ended so much of what
I didn't know in the ghost years —
the slow-moving, depressed days

I slept through like a pair
of scissors left in the rain.

News of you finally bled through
the handful of years I taped together
with silence. I imagined you reading
a rain-soaked war saga of near-romance
between the almost beloved and the impulsed
lover; how he went back to puppeteering
and she to being severe, lovely, older
and untouched. How she would have loved
him "if only his ears were a little more
red, his left eye, a blink softer"
and died believing she never had.
How an off-white evening jacket tried
to fool the moon into believing
that one night is an unbending river
leading somewhere I awakened.

Wonder

This is not the first time hope
left me at the train station waiting

for danger to arrive. We all have
memories and words that mean more

than any others like glances
between new lovers stranded at

a party where the hosts heap agony
and small talk onto everyone's plate.

Maybe there's more between us
than fingers softened into gesture —

a deaf man signing *do you want
to make love* on his wife's belly

in the dark. Yesterday began
with the same worried light now

absent covering the floor, a pair
of women's shoes by the refrigerator,

the smell of coffee almost made.
The right tools and enough

patience, could make that picture
a life. Final, severe happiness.

Repetition

One last story about the years
    I promised not to commit to memory.
    This one wears the same pants,
torn shirt and in the mirror
appears clean shaven, unwrinkled
and tired. Believes it believes
in nothing. Falls asleep each night
revising its last inspired words
I've had enough.
Fifteen years
and cities later, I awakened.
What I remembered is negligible.
What I remember is merciless:
third floor rooms furnished
with strained views of railroad
tracks, the alarm clock chasing
itself around the room yelling fire,
fire, the sun coaxing angry muscles
into black lace up shoes and blue
razor-creased slacks. Teeth brushed
bloody. The same wrong turn each
morning at the top of the stairs.
Staring out of the corporate lunchroom
window, realizing I was lost.
And six

hundred miles later at my parent's
house, throwing a sleepless coat
in my old bed before disappearing
into the attic. Rags of sunlight
rubbing dust from broken picture
frames, my grandfather's rusted guns,
three generations of war uniforms
and wedding clothes. A newspaper
clipping unfolding like a hand
escaping from prayer. The picture
of a newborn wrinkled in its palm.
According to the caption, me. Hours old.

Angels

"Sometimes we Angels look down on Man and envy you."
Martin Scorsece's The Last Temptation of Christ

Back again and again, tired
and trying. Gold sodden wings
limp around his other arms and heart.
Her hair tranquil on the pillow.
He remembers watching her undress.

The brown curve of her shoulder,
arrhythmia of her heart,
rounded bones and muscles,
the shadow of her breasts.

"It all falls apart according to plan."

The first things:

Ten thousand seasons before ice,
opened wings, the invention of fire.

One foot in three worlds.
Scissors cut paper wraps rock.

Streetlights and the sliver-yellow moon
rest their hands on her shoulders.

The last syllable of that evening's prayer
crosses his lips.

In shop windows: faces,
TVs, the world repeating itself.

Stars gnaw at the windows.

Mirror

Between the twice-dumb heart and dead
    August heat, everything: a day,

    a day, a day, a day. Prayers sweat sheened,
a raindrops' skeleton

tattoos the window. Art, Art, where-
fore art? Wherefore you? Where?

Like a mirror photographing a mirror, nothing is
as nothing does. Life being

what it is,
one dreams of revenge.

Upstairs

The usual business.
    Sunday. Almost noon.
    Gin-glazed light.
Window blinds like loose ties in the wind.
Your neighbor screaming *get the hell
out of this room* at his children.
His wife still cocooned in sleep.
Their telephone (it might not be working) doesn't ring.

The radio's slow leak of economics,
weather, afternoon beach traffic,
the withering of this and that
and how to avoid despair.
This is your life:
a wire hanger mourning a white shirt,
thinning gray slacks,
the button in the right suitcoat pocket,
a shoelace too short to tie.

Everything where it should be.

You stir.
I take my coat and go.

Ex Libris

Voices reddened by laughter and Drambuie,
    sun-rubbed windows, an absence of wind —
    those days were spiced to look more substantial.
Everything between us was about you:

how sleep twisted your hair, the dark brown
adventure of your eyes when awakening,
would the weather between here and
the subway ruin your looks for the day.

Your letter — *If only we'd foreseen what
we know now don't take it so on the chin.
Terrible things have happened to us all.
I never intended anything more than soft*

passion arrived in a red envelope
postmarked Iceland and showered my feet
with blue stars. The early months
of your absence wrinkled my hands

into cardboard statues of prayer. By May,
when the tulips and afternoon light seemed
personal again, I adopted Picasso's motto:
When you run out of red, use blue.

Today, while packing box after box
of books I've read and forgotten, letters
from friends who no longer have faces,
the next-door neighbor's radio whines

What's He Doing In My World.
The late afternoon streetlights
coaxed like despair between houses
flicker on and off in confusion.

Art Gallery Pension

To understand Greek architecture,
    look first at human nature.
    The usual weights and measures
mean nothing here: talents,
16 kilos per; water, 37 cents
per liter and a half; even
money is light and unfettered.
An afternoon like this, light
granting shadows overweight
personalities can lead a bus
astray, souring all the passengers,
making the tour guide's monologue
algebraic jazz. The Greeks invented
donuts the size of talents
and a mythological system so elaborate
that when laid flat it resembles
Daedalus' labyrinth at Knossos.
One eyebrow raising another,
this is how to appreciate beauty.

Geography goes watery before
turning blue. If you go far
enough away, another door,
another year and a week,
this is where you'd be staying.

There's a telephone, untranslatable
phrases passing by your door,
photographs of intriguing strangers
littering your wallet. *Would you
come here if your life was in flames?*
Socrates asked questions like that.
"*Woke up like going to heaven because
the flame went out in my stomach.*"
That's the danger of this kind
of light: of always being on the verge
of the marvelous or unexpected beauty,
of exposing the seams where the sky
marries the horizon. *Think of where
we might have been* — that's where
most of us live — between tomorrow
and a week from next Tuesday
on a street lively with tourists,
surrounded by postcards memorializing
architectural ruin and beach erosion.
We lacked nothing of consequence:
only language and inoffensive gestures.

The waiter delivers the house special,
wine splashes against the glass,
another day dissolves into snapshots
of sunsets and local color. Will they
come out up to snuff as illustrations
of enchantment and terror?
Or merely square with our memories?
You never really return from where
you've been — having left a notebook,
an eye for bad news, a postcard
for someone you hope to know better.

"We've grayed a little, but we're still
recognizable. Last time we came here,
I had the board meeting; Kathy came
along and shopped her brains out.
I didn't know you were here.
Maybe next time, Bob."
To travel is to shop. To travel
is to loot; to set the table
for a small miracle. Today
it's Greece again: honey-thick
light, a hand waving away objections.
"*My English is not the best —*
spend your money in my shop."
Nothing much matters in this light.

Travelling Light

Last night, I dreamed of burning cars.
    Clouds shredding the sky.
    Full and bitter, the moon skulking
over water anxious for boats, motion,
curisteptic light. Something soft
and unlit rolling over inside
a yellow Carolina house, glaring
at the alarm clock and disappearing

sixty miles south of Staunton, Virginia
in a red Ford with bald tires while
the architecture of the universe —
unbent wires, yellow howls, a cigarette's
brief, orange constellation —
untangled in front of my car.

Traveling By Albatross

Language gone awry, uncomfortable,
 Rube Goldberged. Hello

 Toledo; not Spain,
but Ohio's broken rivers

and cities longing to spawn. My dream?
To become a fist punching holes

in water, a flightless water bird.
Now you tell your story.

Ah, to be a butterfly –
this is what I learned

leaning against the wind
whose advice I mimic whilst I work

Another Page Illustrated By Fire

Lacking a voice to invent the usual
 suspicions, a door open to the light

moving through like spring wind,
this is how I'd construct it:

no walls or windows, only holes
and white, infinitely white furniture.

The language simpler:
muscles, linguistics, pathology,

the condition of memory.
One man's story is another's

erased memory. "There's something
for each of you out there."

This is family.

Bones Covered With Breath

The moon prays for houses dark
with sleep. Three windows over,

a pair of hands sorts correspondence
and photographs into soft categories.

*Let me come home, please leave the door
open* was yesterday's telephone message

for the wrong number; apologies
addressed to a name absent

from your mailbox are mistakes
a mirror might make. I should

have left a light on in the kitchen,
a glass of milk as an offering

to the quiet that arrives ahead
of you — there wasn't time.

The stars exhausted all the music
they know accompanying the moon.

This explains what's left.

Necessary Angels

Loss gives way to a peculiar lightness:
    a hand clutching water, air

    taking on varietal colors. One year
turning its face into another.

The soft days in Paradise.
"If you could have anything

you wanted, what would it be?"
To float just above ground, inches

over matter: a feather for one
wing, as the other, its shadow.

Hourglass-Memory

The once-perfect and perfumed man's image
    etched against a mirror,

    but not as dead as he should be. The others?
The misremembered, the lonely

unto death, the abandoned, the invisibly hurt,
all harshly eliminated. Memory

like an hourglass, a long, slow accumulation,
grain by grain. Almost always

wrong, and also painfully true.+

The Music Dreams Make Of Empty Rage

Last night in an alcoholic's raw tenor,
    my neighbor sang sentimental radio songs
    and prayed to the walls to hold us all.
The city's dirty, scattered lights
slow danced like cigarette embers
and whispered our names
until again this morning, we rose.

Insomnia Meditation

The midnight trucks haven't yet
    disappeared unlit into this new day.
    The moon's version of the future
I promise to be attentive to everything
scrawled over tomorrow on the kitchen
calendar. The first bones of light
grow restless in the houses of
the dead, the failed, the still living.
a hand seeking an absent face
thinks itself into a fist. Aroused
by the first instructions of light,
the clock radio's ticking voices,
replace the soft beating of wings
once removed from our backs.

Initiation

Her smile, distant highway traffic, and wind obscured moonlight. Her heart, moon-lit, slivered. The remembered street you pull from your pocket and try to open.

Divergent Perspectives

Eagles play percentages. Disregard the metaphysics, evolution. Preened,

    heart imagined wisdom, light, wisdom. Action/reaction equal and opposite. Each part right enough,

still. *Nothing, there was nothing, so I went back.*

Tired again, tired and trying. Wing-muscles raw
against his shoulders. Gray, resting.

One foot in three worlds: the one he did not make, the one
Just beyond his shoulder, the one Beloved absence.

What would he give? Remembers an eagle riding thermals, circling.

The Distance Between Memory And Remembering

The sun replaces last night's clutter.
    not wanting to make up
    with anyone, bent back-
wards and indifferent as the dying rose
on the kitchen table.
whose petals refused to open.
It will be seven years
before this dissolves into laughter and loud talk
among newly-forged friends
about years lost
in too much thought.
He wished for her happiness
The first nights' full moon, then ripped
out the telephone
after calling Cambridge, Trieste, and Munich
where no one was home.
By late morning, a voice he
mistook for hers
filled the room. And if he
hears it again, he swears he'll answer.

Business Travel

To say he had met her, would be wildly optimistic. He saw her, maybe even believed he'd brushed against her and had spoken some words that were lost before they could find her. He had been walking to his car after buying a few groceries: cat food, coffee, light cream and some cookies. It was cold, snow was coming later that day and he wanted to avoid it. He was looking for his car and noticed a woman slumped over in the front seat of her car. He stared for a moment, and then walked over toward the car. As he got closer, he noticed she was crying. Such an intimate act, crying. He was bewildered, uncertain as to whether or not he should do anything other than find his car and leave.

He walked up to the car, hoping that she'd seen him. Would know he understood her tears and wanted to interrupt them, if only for as moment. When he noticed she was looking at him, he froze. He tilted his head to the left and stuck out his lower lip the way a disappointed child does. Then he hugged himself. She was still crying, but a momentary and luminous smile crossed her face. In that sliver of an instant, he wanted so badly to touch her, to hold her and let her cry while being comforted. That is what he imagined. As quickly as their eyes met, she collapsed back into crying.

Later he would tell the woman sitting next to him on the plane about the woman he'd seen earlier that day, and how he'd wished he could have comforted her. The woman sitting next to him smiled warily, anticipating an assault of friendliness ending in an invitation to diner, a tour of the city, a movie, awkwardness at parting, a desire for intimacy. He looked out the window and soon fell asleep. She studied his face, his large hands folded at rest on his legs. When the plane was landing, she asked him if he'd like to go to dinner. Sure, he said, somewhat surprised. When they got up to her room after dinner, bringing another bottle of wine with them, she fumbled for the key. When they got into the room, she turned to him and kissed him. He started to cry disconsolately. He asked her to hold him. He imagined she was the woman he'd seen sitting in her car, crying. And how badly he wanted to comfort her earlier and couldn't.

Migration

You looked for her everywhere
and then came here. This was where

the car broke down. Snow rinsed
moonlight and foot-numbing cold.

Well-lit houses going on and
On and no one home. Her

ripped smile, shotgun dark eyes
and hair. Trash and snow paved

streets, cars burned black,
houses held together by threads

of TV and streetlight. Shadows
voices, made up. Your arms,

birds frozen between flight
and landing. Her sweater,

a scarecrow, failing to empty
a field of three crows.

Darkness, sliding off their wings.

Emergency Lane

They had no voices left. He drove. If she held the baby tightly enough, she knew it would cry. It's hadn't breathed in nearly an hour. He wanted to make love to her and thought about pulling off the road, knowing there'd never be another time.

Triptych: The Art Of Perspective

1. View From The Kitchen

—

One cloud. Enough music
from the only bird in the only

tree. After that, night
and cars. Freshly folded

laundry. Doors, but not opened.
Voices. The TV still the TV.

Another plant staring out
the window. A pair of brown

shoes. A damp shirt balled
against the back of the chair.

2. The Walls Recollect Last Night's Party

—

Does using someone's name
hasten their appearance.

It would be terrible if somebody
at work discovered that I'm an artist.

Anybody can make lunch
and put it in quotation marks.

I had to pull the guy out
of there. He was going

to work like that the bottom
of his car in flames.

3. Transcription

—

If here, then say so.
If not there or here, where.

Is this what matters this.
Water green water green brown.

Noise the stink of it. Air.
Less serious. Lower. Air.

What else. What is it. What what.
What is what what. What.

Making Up The World

In awe and astonishment, we regain ourselves in this world.
There is no other.
— Charles Wright, from "A Journal of Southern Rivers"

Night after night, the dead resume our names,
recite poorly worded memories, shadowbox dreams.

Improper, awkward light pauses at windows, and leaves
night-scraps behind before letting us go.

But that's not what I wanted to tell you.

———————————

In 1955, ten years under the Bomb,
thirty-seven years before constellations

of cigarette smoke on an early morning streetcorner
explained what I meant to the world,

one year and a Tuesday before
the next time I'd die,

two months early, awakened in my mother's womb.
And head first, blood-glazed, one eye

open, to impatient light, rubber hands explaining how
to breathe, the helmet head

caul my first thought,
as I entered this world.

———————————

If there is another, a blue prayer
in a full moon, it came

from my smiling wooden Buddha,
a left-handed illusionist,

whose smile is stars beaten yellow.

———————————

If there is another world, it is raft-nation of *El Dorado*,
stalled on the Amazon. Emperor Lope

de Aguirre, the *Wrath of God*, tells a monkey he grips
by the neck *We'll endure*

imagining himself God's invention of death.

———————————

If there is another world, a ghost looming
misspelled threads and lost wishes

into vernacular rage, failed hands,
misshapen words,

whose unwanted memories, start their annual reawakening.

If there is another world,
it's Illinois, Michigan, Ohio,

Connecticut, North Carolina, New Hampshire,
Massachusetts, Greece and Turkey.

Sleep and stars going the wrong direction.

Another night and the world's on fire. The last
stars are thin, thinner, ash gray

and nothing. Down the street, a saxophone player
unravels another story of loss.

The first song offers a dark rose,
laced with snow and failure.

The second, traces and retraces five
empty fingers of speech.

The third croons the unrequited longing
of my bruised, inarticulate

heart, sewn against my chest,
folded wishes to dream

the scars and veins, back into the body.
Arms discolored, unwashed

by prayer, make up the world

Notes

- **Always Begin Where You Are**: The italicized text in Section 3 is taken from Walter Lowrie's translation of Soren Kierkegaard's The Sickness Unto Death.
- **Two Sides Of The Same Fence**: The last three lines of Section 3 are taken from Stephen Berg's poem, "In The Park".
- **Mirror:** The last three lines are a quote by Paul Gaugain.
- **Art Gallery Pension** is for Karen Bjorkman.
- **Name That Tune** is for Zeynep Beykont.
- **Making Up The World** is for Lori Byrne.

www.ingramcontent.com/pod-product-compliance
Lightning Source LLC
LaVergne TN
LVHW051711080426
835511LV00017B/2848